Unfathomed Secrets

By Parvinder Nagi

The text of this book is set in Georgia 12 points and 1.0 line spacing.

First Edition, 2025
Published by Parvinder Nagi
Available worldwide through Amazon and other major book retailers.

Nagi, Parvinder
Unfathomed Secrets / Parvinder Nagi
ISBN 97983-16253-319

Cover design and edited by Manpinder Singh Nagi

156 Pages

I dedicate this book

UNFATHOMED SECRETS

to my beloved mother
Mrs. Amar Kaur Sandhu
born and raised in Mombasa, Kenya, East Africa.

The woman who gave me my voice just celebrated 98 years of
grace, strength, and love, on 5th April 2025

To my loving mother with all my heart
whose wisdom shaped my understanding of life.

The best gift I could ever give to my mother
on this 'Mother's Day' to last until eternity with glory to God.

Thank you for being my mom.

This book is yours!

TABLE OF CONTENT

FOREWORD

I take immense pleasure and joy in presenting the first collection of poetry, *Unfathomed Secrets*, by the esteemed poetess Parvinder Nagi from India.

Parvinder is a multifaceted author—a talented and gifted soul, an experienced educator, a principal of prestigious Senior Secondary Schools, and an innovator in pedagogical approaches.

While reading the poems of this eminent poetess, it is not erroneous to remark that William Wordsworth's observation in the *Preface to Lyrical Ballads*, where he states that poetry is a "spontaneous overflow of powerful feelings, recollected in tranquility," resonates deeply. These words ring true as we encounter the splendiferous spontaneity and sublimity that define this heart-touching collection.

This beautiful and highly educated lady, with her love for both pedagogy and innovation, entered the magical world of poetry by God's will. During her visit to England, she toured the Museum dedicated to the great poet William Wordsworth.

In those hallowed rooms, she felt a magical, rapturous connection. A divine revelation stirred her soul, and she realized that this world of marvelous poetry was also hers. From that moment on, she immersed herself in the timeless essence of poetic creation, living in the magic of poetic expression.

Parvinder writes with passion, as demonstrated in a national poetry competition that brought together over 2,000 poets from across

India, where she was honored among the top one hundred. This significant achievement confirmed her literary talent and gave her the strength and incentive to continue walking boldly through the world of poetry.

Unfathomed Secrets is her first collection, a work into which she has woven her heart and soul with love and enthusiasm. Her poems are the music of the heart and the speech of the soul, expressing various facets of life and conjuring emotions ranging from happiness to sorrow, employing a vivid array of styles and themes.

Among these is the poignant poem "My Empty Chair." Here, Parvinder delves into the transience of life, capturing the inevitable pain that wounds every soul. Through the verses, she expresses the fleeting nature of life with such grace and calm, making it a pearl in this collection. "My stories untold, my songs unsung, the birds will sing my blues and the winds will caress my empty chair."

In "Life's Tapestry," tenderness is woven into life's intricate fabric. The poem is a delicate and soothing piece that intoxicates readers with its emotional depth.

Parvinder also explores themes of femininity, the abuse of women, peace, and war. Her revolt against the evils of the world is evident, yet much of her work is dedicated to love—the very essence of life. The beauty and charm of her poetry are reflected in her love verses, which gently caress the souls of her readers.

In "Loving You in Millions of Ways," she beautifully pens: "In this stillness of night, isn't there so much to share? In how many ways have I loved you! Like an ancient tale, as I dive into the past, perpetual moments we shared"

Each poem is a tacit acknowledgment of the poet's control over form—here, poetry is "form proceeding from thought," rather than mere figural shapes imposed for decorative purposes.
Parvinder's poetry invites readers to deconstruct, reinterpret, and revel in the pleasure of unveiling what lies hidden beneath or beyond the verbal textures.

Her dedication to art shines through as she continues to write about love, sadness, joy, and pain. These verses, with their beauty and meaning, touch the hearts of those who are ever eager to love.

For this, Parvinder Nagi deserves applause, emerging as a harbinger of hope, love, and peace—noble virtues that affirm her place as an outstanding literary voice. I wish her great success in her endeavors, with the dedication and aspiration to reach new heights.

More books of poetry will follow, and *Unfathomed Secrets* will shine like a star in the poetic firmament.

-   **Gordana Sarić**, *professor and renowned poetess (Queen of Poetry) from Montenegro*

IV

AUTHOR'S NOTE

Dear Readers

Poetry has always been a way for me to express the inexpressible, to take the intangible emotions and fleeting moments of life and give them form through words. The libraries of my mind are filled with verses that capture the beauty, pain, and complexity of our experiences, and I have always believed that poetry serves as a bridge between the poet and the reader, connecting us through shared reflections and insights.

For me, poetry is the art of distilling vast emotions into just a few lines. It allows us to see the world in its simplest, most profound form—a world where a grain of sand holds the universe, and a fleeting moment can carry the weight of a lifetime. Through metaphors and rhythm, poetry creates a harmony that speaks to both the intellect and the heart.

I have always admired how poetry invites interpretation, offering each reader the freedom to find their own meaning. It thrives on ambiguity, urging us to look beyond the literal and engage with the deeper layers of the human experience.

I hope that the poems in this collection will resonate with you, offering moments of connection, reflection, and inspiration. I look forward to hearing your thoughts and feedback as I continue this journey of self-expression and exploration.

Parvinder Nagi

A PHENOMENAL WOMAN

Embracing the whole world
Confining the universe
Within herself
Nurturing the tender soul
Inside her womb
She's a package of
Unconditional brimming love

A splendor of a mother
Lies in the diversity
A personality so dynamic
A maestro of talents galore

She's a magical poetry
A rainbow on the canvas
Flourishing the reigns of life
An unwavering navigator
A healer of all the woes

Singing lullabies in the cradle of night
Whispering bedtime stories
Baking cakes and making shakes
Encountering every struggle
And triumphs
Reshaping her perspectives

A heart with a deep abyss
Full of forgiveness
With indomitable spirit
Enchantress of symphony

Carrying a prestigious crown
She's a phenomenal woman
Full of mysteries
A God figure
Known as MOTHER!

SCENTED LETTERS

I can still feel the fragrance
Of your perfume
From all the letters you sent

Those scented letters bringing
Unlimited kisses so warm

Touching every curve so beautiful
Freaking the sensations mad

Ahh! how I love the touch of your
Quill so intoxicating

Electrifying my senses so deep
Penetrating into the depths of my skin

Revealing secret tales of love
Each letter carries the bond so strong

Sitting at the window sill
Waiting for the delivery
Of your ink

I could not wait
To lay my hand on it
And go through the read so sweet

Whispering in silence
Reading your three letters "I love you"
To the winds caressing my tresses

Blushing I cherish each word of yours

Anchoring your dreams in portals of my eyes

Finding the dried petals of roses
From the pages of your notes

The time may fade the ink of words
But the stolen moments will always linger

Drowning me in nostalgia
In the depths of my heart

Some dreams tucked away
That I could not express

I miss your golden letters
Touching the core of my heart

For now, we live in the world
Where letters do not exist

The ink of your love is worth preserving
For it has travelled miles across

I'll cherish your letters till my last breath
Sealed with a warm kiss!

PORTALS OF MY EYES

I hide someone
Within the panes
Of my eyes
Sparkling with
Millions of stars
Speaking millions
Of languages
Only if you could read

Transmitting emotions
Through the portals of eyes
Drowning in its intensity
Evoking reflections
Bringing myriads of memories
Stirred through the beauty
Of soul

Hidden are the
Number of stories
Down the oceans deep
Brimming in the eyes
Are the secret desires
And unveiled ecstasies
To admire through serene
And calm sublime feelings

My world lies within me
In there I vouch
My dreams fulfilling
And glowing
Like stars in galaxy
These tiny glimpses

Parvinder Nagi

Transcending love
Through all the barriers
For I hold someone
Deep in the ebullience
Of my eyes.

ONLY IF LOVE COULD BE MEASURED

Ahh, only if love could be measured!
He asked
"How much do you love me?"

I said, "Only if you could count
Mine innumerable heartbeats
Or keep an account of my breaths"

Tell me, is love not holding
Each other in the moment of grief?
To be gratified when all is well
Like Autumn breeze
Caressing unendingly
Through the trances
Like the fragrance
In the zephyr
The willows permeating scents
Rivers flowing perpetually
Clusters of galaxies
Chords of the Universe
Calmness of the night
Depths of the sea
The greatest treasures ever

Love is not illusions
Or fairy tales
It is an entity
You reciprocate to
Forgive and be resilient

Love keeps dwelling
For there's no yardstick

Parvinder Nagi

Measuring MY love
From ages past, present and forever

Now tell me

Can YOU measure
My love for THEE?

UNTIL THIS LIFE ENDS

Mystical web spun in the mingled paths so beautiful
Memories of the past journey we walked through
Our sweet nights mesmerizing under the galaxies enchanting
Love began under the stars
Brimming through the breezes swift

Silently you stepped in through the brightest of moonlights
Holding onto the desires overflowing in emotions deep
Dreaming joyous dreams in the world of ecstasies
Fiery echoes, night trysts under the shadows dark

Love's greatest truth wrapped in the divine azures
Rests in thy bosom of the celestial skies so magnificent
Intoxicating by the fragrances of your tresses so beautiful
I lay in my conscious celebrating every thought of yours

Touching my senses through the feelings so vibrant
I would love to embrace you till infinity
We were destined to meet in this birth what may
And our souls never to part until this life ends.

DEFINING MY LOVE

Where do I store my brimming love?

Dew drops of my love
Keeps penetrating through
The intensive emotions

Boundless are the elevations
Of my love
Like empyrean curve scattered with stars

Rising and falling
Are the ebbs of my heart
Singing the notes of my love so true

My heart is full of gala tales
Amidst millions of enduring trails

Mine endless love keeps dripping
Unfurling the truth, it holds

Defining my love
Are the few metaphors

Not prose nor poetry
Can compose my love

As my love is a treasure
Within the box full of pleasures

My love resonates
With every breath so warm

Can you not hold
Mine love so divine!

GLACÉD NIGHTS

Resonating to the
Spun memories
Of our glazed nights
When ecstasies began
Under the stars
And brightest of moonlights
Holding onto that image
It is joyous dreaming dreams
Fiery echoes, night trysts
And pleasurable screams

Love's greatest truth
Rests in thy bosom
Playing the soft rhythms
Carrying memoirs of love
Dancing as rhythmic thunders
Illumining the untamed love
Caressing the palpitation
Of senses

Abandoned to the sails
The rants we had
The chapters never forgotten
For every moment that passes
Leaves sparks so misty
The stories we spun
Beautifully woven
Through the souls
Never to part.

LOVING YOU IN MILLIONS OF WAYS

In this stillness of night
Isn't there so much to share?

In how many ways
Have I loved you
Like an ancient tale
As I dive into the past
Perpetual moments we shared
Loving you in millions of ways
All the odds making us indestructible
Every time I think of you
Leads me down the poetry lane

Have I not treasured you in zillion incarnations?

Piercing the darkness of night
Penetrating deep in the heart
You have a place
Which no one could fill
Yes, memories are precious
But I never wished to live
In reflections with you
I grieve
You had never gone

May I ask if you never charred in the agony of lust?

Only if you reminisce
We loved under the skies so blue
We hugged through the glittering stars with emotions deep

You touched my soul
Through words so warm
I yearn for you evermore
With the age-old pain

Can you not feel my
Limerence for you?

Though miles apart
You are loved indescribably
In numerous forms
Our love is inscripted
In every age
In every life
My love will never fade
Nor can it be erased
For there is lots more in store

Could we not reacquaint just once again?

If I could build a bridge
I would walk the path
Bringing you back
And never letting you go
Snuggled in my arms
Till infinity.

THE BLEEDING INK

Swiftly when I hold my pen
The bleeding ink
Finds you in every word
For now, you live
In every bliss of my sentence

Reading the commas
Filling in the blanks
No full stops could ever bring
The end to our story tales

No question marks are found
In the pathways we walk
Holding on to the semi colons
Here so we move on

Until the dreams do part us, Alas
Here we stand with support
Of exclamation
Does anything matter if we live closed
Secure in apostrophes

If you let me write
You will find all the answers
To your whys
Let us breathe in the capital
Of every endeavor we begin

Until we find our destination
We may pause many a times
Punctuating through
The songs of our life

Proceeding with caution
We can walk through the
Aging of lines
Adding more glory
With three dots across

When fears are eradicated
No ellipses are needed
Yes, I am skeptic
Yet you can read me
With hyphen and dashes
In between the lines

In clauses and brackets
In a new paragraph
I will rewrite you swiftly
When I hold my pen.

SEDUCTIVE SONNETS

In the silken tapestry of my thoughts
I live in the solace depths of your longings
Finding you in the verses of my ink
Embracing you in the shadows of my nights

Where ambers of my heart play its melodies
Caressing the pain with its soothing balm
Reciting on my heart the seductive sonnets of love
Kissing in wilderness between the urges
Of my breath so deep

Drowning in the portals of your eyes so drowsy
Igniting the flames of lust
Glittering like the sprinkles of the stardust
I write you over my poetry again and again.

FOR I AM A POETESS

If you ever fall in love with me
I will write you in my thoughts
And keep you alive
In the jottings of my lines
I will make you breathe
In the stories past

If you ever fall in love with me
Every morning
I will paint your world new
You will be hummed
In every lyric of my verse
Entwined your heart with mine
Will never let you fall apart

If you ever fall in love with me
You will find yourself
In every read of my page
Knotted in every word sensuously
Mingled beautifully
Weaved in mystic love notes

If you ever fall in love with me
The ink of my pen
Will spread your beauty
Through the love ecstasy
To live in the bliss of my pages

If you ever fall in love with me
You would plunge
In fascination of words
Twinkling in the transformation

Of scintillating world
In the slumber of poetic dreams

For, I am a poetess!

UNEXPECTED MIRACLE

How beautiful is to find
Someone crossing your path
With cascading elated vibes

As if something precious
You relate to
A fascinating thought
Someone has left you
Lingering with

Experiencing the sleepless night
For someone
Not getting off your mind

So many questions
I am left wondering with
Yet a stranger
But seemed so convincing

Known for few minutes
Imbuing with impression
With a beautiful adieu
Journey ended before it started

When you find someone
Permeating your senses

Is that not an unexpected miracle?

MAY I ASK?

May I ask
If you would love to amble with me
Through the vistas so beautiful

Love is a bliss unspoken
Soaring high above the zenith blue
Embracing you through my eyes
Every time I pause
I think of you

Deep in my heart
Caressing your love
With firm determination
Each passing day
I hold you so swiftly

Whispering your name
Ripples every drop of blood
Kissing the tender lips
Flooding with emotions
Is my divine love

You are the promise
Of my new beginnings
We sing the duet
Of mystic melody
Again, and again

Conquering your heart
With graceful gestures
Are the blooming scents
Of wild emotions

Parvinder Nagi

Embedded In love

Let me choose the threads
And weave them
Into poetry
Intoxicating slowly
As you read the verses

The beautiful tapestry
Of words are
Intricately mingled
With cascades of elegance
For next to you is
Where I belong.

DID I EVER GO SEEKING FOR YOU

You know my cravings
Very few are chosen
By my tender heart
And loved so very deeply
Holding your thoughts

Wobbling to be held by your warmth
Once more
Under the moony light
I sit gazing at the stars
Waiting for the answers
To my unsolved puzzles

The sacred relation
I have connected with you
Eternally we are destined
For the unconditional love
Yet, that fear of losing you
Gives me goose bumps!

Can you lose something precious that's yours?

I am just minuscule
And you full of wisdom
A master of crafted gems
I wonder if I fit into your frame of
Poetry

Why am I connected to your path?
Did I ever go seeking for you?
Was I ever incomplete before this?

Parvinder Nagi

This silence is comforting me
Reflecting back
Exactly what my soul
Is looking for!

I WILL CHOOSE YOU AGAIN AND AGAIN

I choose to walk every
Pace with you
In hundreds of lifetimes
I will choose you
Again, and again

Over the mountains
Where the butterflies wander
I will choose you
Again, and again

For each milestone
Has its own story
I see myself living with thee
I will choose you
Again, and again

There is so much to unfold
Woven in its own tapestry
In new patterns of life
I will choose you
Again, and again

I treasure each moment
That mystery unravels
In hundred decades
I will choose you
Again, and again.

GIFT OF LOVE

Do I possess a special
Gift for you?

Yes, here's a gift of love
And the trust till eternity
Nothing more precious to give
But a gift of understanding

Through the lost times
A little empathy for the moments
We spent together
A gift of strong bonds
With strength so divine

The gifts of joy and happiness
For the times we shared
The moments of solitude
And resilience

Here's a gift of love
A love that's deep and pure
A love that's immeasurable
A love that's most precious

The warmest relationship
We accomplish
A gift to cherish through the ages
I renew my heart
Sharing the love I possess.

BALLET OF THOUGHTS

I have whispered your name
Through the pine trees
For the fear of getting lost
I have engraved your name
On the leaves too

I have breathed you
With every breeze
I have cuddled you in my thoughts
Loved through the mossy hooves
In beautiful dreams

Through my shadows
I have seen you walking
Besides me
Floating in deep love
Jotting your name
On every cloud

Through the propeller of time
Never letting me grow old
Your elegance of thoughts
Keep dancing in my mind.

POETIC GLEAMS

Searching the answer in every touch of yours

How often do I gaze into your eyes
Unveiled through the darkness
The sublime connection we make
Feeling the depths of true love

Is there any answer to the love's timeless dreams?

I wonder in this poetic gleams
Where the soul is free
The quill of our heart
Writes the verses of love and tender care

Merging in the love story for eternity
Searching the love entwined
Fleeting in the gentle breeze
Love exists
where our story begins.

LET ME HOLD YOU

Let me hold you swiftly
Like the morning rays
Caressing the lilacs and violets
Stars kissing the blanket of night
Following the sweetness of silence

Holding you like the strings of orchestra
With sensuous feelings
Symphonies of ecstasies
The touch of tenderness
Concerto of midnight tunes

Pulsating the heartbeats
Embracing in my arms
Gently touching your senses
Giving meaning to my wildness
You complete my poetry.

WHISPERS OF MY LOVE

Touched with endless emotions
I listen to the whispers of love
With miraculous burning desires
Following the light of lamps

We are drifting
Under the same sky
Miss not the messages
I sent through the stars

Stirring up the feelings
Every time they shine
Upholds the emotions
Blending the moments

Twinning the hearts
Defying the darkness
Filling the emptiness
With endless emotions

Walking away in delight
With bounty and grace
Listening to the
Whispers of love

For we are together
Walking through the
Sparkling lights
Of magical cravings.

CASCADING TRESSES

Misty fragrance
Of the morning breeze
Playing tunes of eloquence
Soaking its misty essence
New romance is brewing
In the meadows lush green

For I have fallen in love
With your cascading tresses
Floating under the azure sky
Caressing through the
Infinite horizons

Exuberant is the beauty
Of your coiffures
Brushing across
The curves of your face
With the scents of
Morning breeze.

GRACIOUS WOMAN

You may brush off the colors
From the canvas of my life
Yet, I will keep painting even brighter

May I ask if my walking with pride bothers you?
For I walk like I own
The pearls of the ocean

You may dig hurdles
But I will move on indefinitely
Like the flow of a river

May I ask you if my status lets you down?
For, I walk on heels, that are higher than your standards

You may tread me in the dark
Still, I will knock down
Every barrier to move on

May I ask if you envious my beauty?
For, even the moon
Hides in the clouds at my glance

Just like the sun rises and the stars twinkle
I will keep shining and rising
Again, and again

For I am a gracious woman.

ENTWINED WHISPERS

How deep are the echoes
Of your whispers
Not everyone can understand
For the language of whispers
Is only known to you and me

I can count on the measures
Of your whispers
As they speak louder
Than the words
Our whispers are entwined
Deep down the heart
I hear your whispers
In the gushes of storms
Each of your word wrapped
In the music of wind

The warmth of your whispers
Are the vibes of ecstasy touching my skin
How I want you to keep repeating
Your whispers are an exuberant miracle

You touched the core of my heart
Through the ink of your pen
Every word you write
Is engraved on my heart
Bringing soul whispers to me
I conquered you at first sight
You are one of the best miracles
I have experienced in a true sense
I admit and say on a high note
It is a love that is so soothing

Full of empathy
The unspoken promises
Only our heart knows
You dwell deep in my thoughts
Hopefully, time allows us to stand
For each other with respect and grace

That glimpses and glance of your wit
Word plays with your physical elegance
Flaring and floating
In ambience of your beautiful heart
Warm and imbibed
With your pretty alluring
And wooing vibes

Here I found
Nesting an attachment
To stay in your ethereal vanity
Yes, this is a kind of love
And I concur this to say that
I anchored with that esteem sublimity
And feel pride in saying
love Is love
An unsaid whisper
That cannot be touched
But we blossom and bloom together

I confess these entwined whispers

Are you and me
That maketh us.

IF YOU CHOOSE

If you choose to read
The poems of my heart
Walk by me through the roughest storms
Engulfing and wading through the torrent waves

If you choose to read
The poems of my heart
Pave your way merging
Through my thoughts
Pick up the unspoken words
Drenching yourself in the sad notes

If you choose to read
The poems of my heart
Submerge in my emotions
And come live in the
Fantasies of my dreams
Rolling down the tears
Of love soliloquy

If you choose to read
The poems of my heart
Come taste the wine of my love
The tempestuous stories lay here
That I have weaved

Wait not

Just read me!

BEWITCHING ELEGANCE

Ah! she wore peony in her silken hair
Gentle like the petals fresh
Bathed in the scents of fragrances
Nurtured in delicacies
To enliven her mind
Assorted with grace and love
Carrying magical secrets in her eyes

She walks in beauty through mystical silence
Unfurling secrets of her sparkling beauty
Bewitching elegance embracing the mystic night
The silvery moonbeams kissing her lips so passionately

She is a timeless symphony
Like a dew drop of pearl on the petals so soft
A magical wand on the propeller of dreams
An epitome of grace like an old bottle of wine
Intoxicating my senses so divine
Her fragrance penetrates through the skin of my body
Luminescence testament of beauty she is.

MELTING SENSATIONS

Restoring and replenishing
Slipping into oblivion
Are the skies
With the diamond
Jewels dropping down
Celebrating renewed life

Would you not love the fragrance
Of dampened air spreading love under the blue azures?

Where the love exhilarates
Entwining between two souls
Kissing passionately
Through the sublime
Cascades of gushing breathes
So pure and warm

Begins the saturation
Of love under
The umbers blue
Penetrating through
The senses of mind
Capturing each emotion

Season of winter
Celebrations entering
With bounties of warmth
Inviting lovers
To flaunt in romance
Bathed in passion

Drenched in blissful delight
With jubilations
Of millions of
Sparkling ecstasies

Parvinder Nagi

Touching the zenith
Above the glories beautiful

Flurry breezes escalating
Through the trances
Of waving strands
Blushing and smiling
Overwhelmed in
Mutual conscience

Melting sensations
Propelling thoughts
New paths drenched
In intoxication
Mussing cuddles
Enlightening the souls

Who would not love to
Merge in this melting romance

URGE OF LOVE

In a moment of bliss
Where there lies
No boundaries
Upsurges the
Urge of love

Chanting gloriously
A heavenly melody
Wrapped in
Profound validations
With Infused euphoria

Extending MY hand
To yours on silent notes
For only once
I will pass this
Path crossing YOURS!

Parvinder Nagi

UNFOLDED MYSTERIES

Watching the sun kissed ripples
In the sea
And approving the dancing waves
In glee

Listening to the soothing rhythm
Of the tides
And splashing through the waves
I go in pride

Loving the musical notes
Of the breeze
And wisps of soft clouds
Sailing across the sky

Whispering softly
Through the unfolded
Mysteries of life
Am striding upon the seashore
Beholding the beauty of nature

Gleaming sunlight
Touching the horizon
Walking across the sands
Leaving behind some footprints

Hence, I love being here
Where the ocean meets the shore
Dwelling in the dreams of love.

CREATING MEMORIES

Along the ocean sand
As we walk hand in hand
As clear as cloudless skies
Looking into each other's eyes

Friendly waves ebb back and forth
With pristine emotions as we go
Brimming with all the bliss
As we two stand and kiss

There is nowhere else I want to be
All my love I have for thee
Wrapped in the warmth of your arms
I walk with you embracing my life

Perpetuating our entwined hands
We walk along the seashore sands
Promises kept are shuddered never
Creating memories to last forever.

CHERISHED CACHE

We now must farewell speak
To the cherished cache
Woven with the golden threads
Through 365 days
Nourishing happy delights
Of the days begone
Letting it go down
The memory lane

Though 'tis sad to bid adieu
O'er the moments we have knitted
Lingering to the fragrances
Whispering softly to the winds
That once did engulf us

Sailed the year gazing through
The windowpanes
Watching the majestic moon
Nurturing the beauty
In the tranquility of mind

Future appears with
A blank sheet of paper
Blooming with new hopes
Our wistful gaze casting
Over the blissful days

Looking upon
The new beginnings
Welcoming another challenge
Through the coming year
Riding us to new glories

WHERE PEACE DWELLS

Peace dwells…
In the beacon of hope
In the gentle breeze
In the rustling leaves
Where lilies bloom
Swaying in the meadows green
Singing of birds on the twigs so sweet
Where the sun shines
Brightening the azure skies

Peace dwells in the giggles of children
Where innocence prevails
It exists in the hearts
Where souls entwine
Intoxicating your senses
With fragrances galore
Leaving you in serenity and solitude

Judging not the colour nor race
Eradicating the shadows grey
Weaving the tapestry of life
Keeping the secrets so fine
Wading through the waves
Dancing in melodious tunes

Splashing through the tides of time
Cuddled in the nature's blessings
Each day with bliss of gratitude
Tuning with the world in harmony
Embracing the warmth of relationships
Let us build peace and harmony
Through the years unveiling the shadows dark.

ESOTERIC DREAMS

Dreams O dreams!
How wondrous is to trace
You down the valleys
So beautiful

Looking up the mirages
Which path do I follow
Changing the world
Manifesting the newest
Of miracles

Illustrations of my soul
Drifting away the
Speculations so exciting
Holding on to illusions
So desperately

A unique thrill unconfined
Down the woods
Predicting the paths
Unknown and bizarre

Collecting one by one
Weaving together
Each night
In my cosy linen
Cuddling in my arms
Are dreams unlimited

Transforming my aspirations
Where my love abides
Holding your hand
With a gush of sigh
Rejoicing warmth of your kiss
Bringing all the bliss

Beautifully swaddled
In a silky linen
Esoteric dreams
Scattering in languishment
Are the pieces
Woven in tapestry.

ELEGANCE OF LOVE

Dancing through the moonbeams so enchanting
Under the twinkling stars in the amidst of challenges
Yet keeping us connected
With firm determination in mind
Waiting with patience and perseverance
For your kisses so warm and sweet
I decorate each ray so magical
Crafted every verse I write
Unparalleled embodiment
Weaving tapestry of dreams
Soaked in the elegance of love
Unravelling the deepest mysteries
Transporting down the abyss of heart
Awakening the soul from slumber's deep
Unfolding the stories untold
Drifting my thoughts where dreams reside
Through the night so inviting
I paint the canvas
Embracing one another
We renew our bond of love
Knitting the web of trust
We mingle in the breathes so warm
Never to let you go
For I live in the sheets
Of crumpled linen
Wrapped in the scents of your body
Where I hear the echoes
Of your silence
Lying under
The twinkling stars.

NEVER TO PART

Here are the memories of our exuberant night
Holding onto the beautiful dreams bright

Where love began under the gaze of stars
Enjoying the night trysts unto the pleasurable strides

Made to live in each other's heart
Destined to meet and never to part

Playing along the magical charms
Nourishing with loves balm

With stirred passions in slumbers deep
Held unto the emotions sweet

Like pulsing embers of wanton yearn
Holding you in my arms firm

ELEVATED ASPIRATIONS

Ambitious to follow her own decorative paths
She is passionate full of zeal and vigour
Rejoices every moment of life making the best of it
Valorous in all the aspects of her life

Nightingale full of love and emotional melodies
Inspiring and influential through her deeds
Desperately fallen in love with her dreams
Crowning herself with love and empathy

Wrapped in Gods divine creation with graciousness
Elevated aspirations with gusto of energizing spirits
Embodiment of divine wisdom
Rejuvenated and rebuilding her magical castles so beautiful.

WILD ECSTASIES

Let me die in the emotions of your love!

Finding treasures of trust
Deep in your heart
Longing for the thrilling secrets
You hold in the gushing tides

The never-ending wild expectations
I see in this paradise
Let my lips taste the salts of your soul
The melody of your ecstasy is enormously infectious

The dreams of lust are wild and mysterious
Lemme find the bliss of my love
Where the sea kisses the shores endlessly
By the passing breeze of awakening love!

Parvinder Nagi

LOST IN YOUR OBSESSION

Embarking on the journey
Touching the willows of my heart
Evoking emotions

Embracing life's beautiful spectrum
Where love looks like a rainbow of hues
Intoxicated by your effervescence

Counting the stars as I recall your name
Witnesses the moon and my world gets transformed
Into the realm of your obsession

In the calm and eloquent moment
I confess my love for you
Mingled in the chasms of our passion.

TRANSCENDS OF SOLITUDE

Here I sit lonely on the windowsill
The nature looks faded in the evening hues
I see a world of thoughts and dreams inside me
My loneliness expressing more than my ink does

I delve into the depths of my serenity
Haunting my own self in quiet moments
Amidst the silence I discover myself
Fighting the battles of my mind

My heart erodes in loneliness
Painting my own canvas
Through the vivid dreams outside the window
Travelling through the vistas unknown

Embracing solitude, I find the unravelling mysteries
I live on the face of the world in
The dark shadows of lonely night

In this stillness I find peace
Learning the lessons of life deeper and more meaningful.

THE LOVE I NEVER CAME ACROSS

You stole every beat of my heart wafting in darkness
Finding you in dreams across the miles
Your arms wrapped around me
With illusions of kisses in a sigh
Disturbing my sleep so deep beneath

You wander in my thoughts like wild ecstasies
Caressing my soul so divine
Your thoughts keep haunting through all the greys
Miss you in hallucinations knowing not why

Baffling with my moods
Awakening from the slumber
Through the dark corners of my room
Invading and unfolding the darkness

Believing the mistaken notions
Diffusing the tangled mess
Drifting through the forbidden echoes
Behind the shadows of illusionary curtains

Missing the heartbeats I long for
Reminiscing the curdles so warm
That I keep dreaming of

I crave for the love
That I never came across

For I live in the illusions so beautiful.

RHYTHMIC BLESSINGS OF PEACE

Choosing peace is all about
Saying lots of goodbyes
For I have learnt
To let go things
That do not
Belong to me

Deeper the pain
If allowed to penetrate
Let go the miseries of past
Do not reach out to me
With your fake promises
Playing gimmicks

I would love to survive
In my own silence I can feel
Peace be my desire
For I am blessed with love
Harmony and rhythmic blessings

Aligned with contentment
Overwhelmed with
Multiple gifts bestowed
Relishing the richness of
His divine grace
Touching my soul
Living in his manifestations

Getting wiser and older
I realize what I must forego
No more battles of mind
I conquer the
Adjustments and acceptances

Just a heart full of

Parvinder Nagi

Gratitude, love and
Peace be mine

Sometimes in letting go
You gain

Sometimes in letting go
You heal the pain

Sometimes in letting go
You set yourself free

Sometimes in letting go
You can choose who to be

Sometimes in letting go
You are gifted

Sometimes in letting go
You find peace

Sometimes in letting go
You feel pride through
Peace and love.

IN THIS SILENCE

Every breath whispering ecstasies
Every syllable touching
The soul so tenderly
Intoxicating scents beneath
The creases of linens
Gentle warmth tickling senses
Echoes whimpering softly
Gazing through the darkness
You're missed
In this silence

Wrapped in rhapsody
Walking in the dark night
Ardently swaying in harmony
Fragrances familiar
Touching the breath
Fastening the heart beats
Embracing your thoughts
Turning the night
So magical
You are missed
In this silence.

Parvinder Nagi

INDESCRIBABLE LOVE

Love is often torn on the edges yet so beautiful inside
Not a fairy tale so easy to be read
Through the pages rumpled and tumbled

Love is indescribable through the ages lived
Love is not love that changes for the lust of its needs
The four letters are often so condensed to be swallowed

Haunting untrodden paths of love
Kissing so gently every curve of the lips
Cuddling in the bed of roses

Yet pricked with its thorns so badly
As every season that comes and goes
Love has to be renewed in times to go

It's enchanting to let go its sorrows
Contemplating the symphony of love galore
Through the brimming desires so warm

Is like stumbling on the glossy floor.

I WAIT FOR YOU

If you are looking for me

I am found in the
Fragrances of Peonies
With quintessential aromas
I am found in the
Oceans deep
As a drop of shining pearl
I am found in the
Air so pure
Stirring through the pines
Across the mountains
I am found in the
Lingering odours
Dabbing my warm breaths
I am found in the
Ecstasies of every heart
Dipped in love
I am found in the
Tranquil woods
In the serene quietness
Of mind
I am found in
All the forms of love
For I delve deep in emotions
I am found in the
Poetry of my silence
Where peace dwells
With longings deep
I wait for you.

Parvinder Nagi

MELODIES OF SOLILOQUY

For once upon a time
You were the throb of my heart
I still feel your fragrance
Under the crisp creases of my linen sheets
Bringing me the warmth of your arms
Touching the deepest chords of my heart

Now I write melodies of soliloquy
All the time carrying you in my mind
My eyes glisten with an unshed tear
It's a joy that's more than a fear
In the deep warm soulful stillness
Loving insanely every bit of you

Between the shadows of joy and pain
The words uttered so wild and weak
In the emotions where madness melts
Cherished are your memories
Today and forever.

RHYTHMS OF HEART

Binding the strings of heart
In mellifluous notes
Singing your name
Embedded in every verse of my poetry
Captivating your emotions
With grace and love
I hear the rhythms of your heart so warm

You will be hummed in every lyric
Of my verse so fine
Painting your world anew
Never letting you fall apart
I assure you for the lifetime
Keeping forever entwined
Your heart with mine

Upholding the emotions thine
Blending the moments sublime
Twinning the hearts
So pure and fine
I will make you live
In the stories divine

Submerging in the mystic
Spirit of my soul
You're the threshold
In the path of my life
My world gets transferred
Into the beautiful realms
As I conquer the treasures
Of your love making me complete.

AN ELOQUENT LOVE

Let's pull a leaf from the nature's book

Where fairies have penned their autographs in tints

Signed on mountains and hills

Borrowed from sunset kisses
And moonbeam lights

Pleasing the haunting souls
Across the prairies vast

Where lilies and daffodils dance
Dwelling in the secret mysteries of past

Revealing the joys of seraphic hearts
Written on every petal so beautifully

Mellowed to the tender light
An eloquent love so innocent

Bringing happiness galore
To every heart it explores.

CASCADING EMOTIONS

A beautiful symphony across the miles
Listening to the rhythms of heart
We meet lying under the same moonbeams
Cascading emotions sublime and pure

Unspoken silence conveying
The messages so divine
Entwining the souls
In the world of dreams
Embracing each other
Through the bonding so strong

Mystical thoughts woven
In the tapestry of love notes
Whispering so gently
The secrets untold
Crossing the boundaries
Through the bridges of realm

The silent quill conveying
The messages so deep
Sailing through the seas
Floating on the waves
Connecting the souls

Kissing the ecstasies of wilderness
Where words silently connect
The language of mind
Listening to each other's heartbeat
Understanding the language of telepathy
Connecting heart to heart.

MISSING HEARTBEATS

Oops!
Can the cardiologist help
Find MY missing beats?

Am I falling in love again?

My heart speaks in a subtle way
Asking if I proclaim
To the month of Valentine

I can see love dripping
From the soul of my heart
Thriving in exuberance

May I ask if this is the month
Full of ecstasies?

Ah! how I love the jingles
That my heart sings
For the one holding
A piece of my heart
From miles apart

Let my cardiologist find
The abyss of my fragile heart
For you live in the depths
Of its warmth

Pulsating and striking
The chords so soothing
Feeling every single
Pulse of yours
From thousands of miles

Fearing the splurge of

Unfathomed Secrets

The missing beats
Echoing your name
Is every leap
Of my heartbeat

Oh! How I relish
Listening to the
Cacophony echoes
Of the heart

For YOU reside deep
Within the cushions
Of my heart

Until I missed the beats
Of my heart
I never knew
In the whimsical odyssey

I am in love

FOR ONCE AGAIN!

Parvinder Nagi

WHEN YOU THINK OF ME

When you think of me
Just jot down your musings
And let me read it

When you think of me
Just jot down your ardour
And let me feel it

When you think of me
Just jot down your cravings
And let me go crazy for it

When you think of me
Just jot down your yearnings
And let me fulfil them

When you think of me
Just jot down your passions
And let me drench in it

When you think of me
Just jot down your silence
And let me listen to it

When you think of me
Just jot down your torments
And let me share it with you

When you think of me
Just jot down your exultation
And let me cherish it with you

When you think of me
Just jot down your ecstasy
And let me celebrate with you

When you think of me
Just jot down your ink
And let me encrypt on my soul

When you think of me
Just jot down your dreams
And let US meet there.

Parvinder Nagi

SEA OF THOUGHTS

Some emotions submerged
In the sea of thoughts

Drifting deeper into
The echoes of melodic verses

My heart is drenched
With the diluted passions

The unsaid words
The unpenned lyrics

That keep swimming
And sometimes drowning

I wish to flood my page
With unseen colours

For you to read me
In silence.

FAIRY TALES SO BEAUTIFUL

Her stories were like fairy tales
Dwelling in the books so beautiful
Where fairies and their
Magical wands lived through the ages
She dwelt in the woods
Stepping through the lilies and daisies
Running after the rabbits and squirrels
Playing peekaboo hiding in the bushes
Living in the handful of time
Her enchantments
Transforming into spells
On the wings of flight
Kissing the snowy mountains
Dew drops plenty and snowflakes white
Over the pinewood trees
Embedded flowers in the golden locks
And fragrances in the air
Fluttering and dancing beneath the trees
Mysterious were her jesters
Stealing hearts with real flaws
And incredible were her qualities
Turn the pages
For she dwells
In the fairy tale stories
So beautiful!

Parvinder Nagi

STROKES OF BRUSH

Not worried
The brush strokes
I have used
Starting my journey
Through this new year

For I have mixed
The colours of hues
From the depths of my heart
Choosing the best brushes
Defying me

I cannot satisfy everyone
Visiting the canvas of my life
The world owes me nothing
I strive hard to shape my life

With every stroke of brush
Creating my own story
Enjoying each moment
This night must give

Full of love and light
Living each moment
Loving this life
To the fullest.

INSPIRING SYMPHONY

Why should I not
Fall in love
With my feet?

Traipsing through
The wading tides
Strolling through
The sands
Leaving behind
The sparkles
Embarked on the
Bays of memories
Enchanting tales
Woven through every step
Making life's
Exquisite cadence
Inspiring symphony
Difficult to put
Into words
Paving every inch
Sauntering from
Me to you

And thus
I would fall in love
With my esoteric feet.

Parvinder Nagi

APOLOGY TO MYSELF

I apologize myself
For the times I was broken
For not a fault of mine

I apologize for the battles
I fought for the sake of others
And never been appreciated

I apologize for all the times
I ignored myself
To please others

I apologize myself
For sacrificing my needs
To fulfill else's demands

I apologize for
Hurting myself
In silence for peace

I apologize for
Tearing my feelings apart
In lieu of compromising

I apologize myself for
Not been able
To express my gratitude

I apologize for
Not able to value my
Worth in time.

LIBRARIES OF MY MIND

Your thoughts have filled
The libraries of my mind

Not seen you ever
Yet my eyes are looking for you

Swept by the tempest of your love
A spirit beautiful and kind

A ghastly wind rushing in
Dragging like autumn leaves

On the floors of my heart
Plunging me in its lust

My senses leaving me deaf
Oh! How I am longing for you

Who are you?

For you have filled
The libraries of my mind.

CONFETTI OF RAIN

Pitter-Patter drizzles the confetti
Imbuing like wild romance
Kissing me everywhere
Soaking in emotions
Singing the melodies of heart
Dancing with every rhythm
Enjoying the musical notes
Under the grey skies
Caressing the locks of my hair
Gliding down the neck
Waves of desire
Ripping through the skin
Bringing warmth of sensation
Embracing the storms of love
Craving the sultry kiss
Dancing in the love ecstasy
Soothing my soul
Nature's bountiful creation
Showers from heaven
Magical ecstasies
Inspiring the writers
With bleeding ink
Jotting the downpour
Of silver pearls
Luring in the mist of air
Defusing into belief
Of esoteric minds
Waiting for you
To wrap me in your arms
Come drench me
In the confetti of your love.

RE-LIVING MEMORIES

Are we not submerged
In the memories past?
Flittering memories beckons in the archives
Like changing seasons
From spring to autumn
And submerging in the winter snow

Reminding some miraculously escaped moments
Enlightening and embracing some good hours
Craving for some mysteries unsolved
Beautiful paths untrodden

Down the memory lane we go again
Memories stuck and dwindled
Reuniting the present to past
Some generous and few precious

Embracing those moments
Yearning for someone special
And some causing aches
Bringing soars wetting pillows

Profound memories forever lasting
Re-living the moments lost
Enlightening and embracing
Cravings for the lust of time gone

Some mysteries unsolved
Beautiful paths untrodden
Down the memory lane are
The haunting memories re-lived.

Parvinder Nagi

LATE ARRIVALS

How annoying are the late arrivals

Arriving too late, of course
Deliveries of my letters
Seems they are coming
Drifting through the lyrical ocean
Folded in the rhythmic waves
Drenched in the melodious verses
Now too late
Moonlit nights alluring into lust
Narrating stories from a poet's pen
Dripping down it's ink
Too late to arrive
Sitting on the windowsill
Desperately I wait here
For the letter not arrived yet
Nevertheless, our love is like a pen
And a paper which is indescribable
Missing those farewell kisses
The heart is sinking
The sunset is prevailing
The gloom is falling

It's too late now
The letter hasn't arrived.

FEMININITY

Like an ornamental piece
She is carved so beautifully
Through every curve so beautiful

Adding to the generations
Creating histories
She moves mountains
And holds the pangs of desires

She is an epitome of grace
Never descending her age
Her limbs often weak
Yet strong pieces of support

She carries a magnificent smile
With ardent charms
She is an ocean of femininity
Like the waves of sea

Only if you are a good swimmer
You may play safe
With every tide of hers
Falling and rising swiftly

She is a fantasy of dreams
Carrying her ambitions
Ever flaunting in her speculations

Be it childhood, youth, or old age
She carries all the stages
Of her life in one baggage.

Parvinder Nagi

STRETCH MARKS

Reflecting a mother's pride
Are the beautiful stretch marks
An autobiography of an
Accomplished femininity

It speaks volumes of
A mother's strength
Profound symbol of fertility
Signs of an everlasting love

Reshaping adorable body curves
The scars of fragmentation
Zigzagging like a wild Tiger
Gained from a labor pain

The crafted verses of poetry
Sketched on the skin
Replenishes the identity
Of a phenomenal MOTHER!

DO NOT STAB HER WITH PAST

Do not confront the woman
For unknown reasons
She had in the past
For being in a broken relationship
Who must have gone through divorce
And for reasons betrayed

Sometimes physically abused
Must have been drugged
Nudity captured shamelessly without remorse
Some must have been tortured
With sexual abuse
And some might have gone
Through suicidal attempts

Do not stab her with past
For she still has not given up
Her hopes to move on
With guilt on her masked face
Wiping her tears with
Grasping promises
For the future not yet seen
Strengthening herself
With the drained energy

Help her move on
With the world today
Making her tomorrows better
For she deserves the love
She has always yearned for
Since ages.

EMBRACING THE FATHERHOOD

Fathers are the unsung heroes of all the times

Embarking on the journey so new
Embracing the fatherhood new
Cuddling his child since birth
With heart so subtle and pure

He is the first love of his daughter
Raised with flair and modesty
Bringing hugs with butterfly kisses
A beacon of hope an anchor so strong

Knowing your deepest fears
Would help you dust yourself off
From wiping the tears of sadness
Damsels saved until the music filled rhymes
Bringing happiness through the wondrous times

Building bridges and fixing the things
Toiling hard in the sun and rain
Unwavering dedication and commitments
Sacrificing through
Life's twists and turns

Spreading the wings of hope
Through the challenges so bitter
Kissing the bruises and aspiring the future
Chasing the monsters and
Soothing the scars

Embracing in his arms comforting the souls
Equipped with tools of life
An unbreakable bond that
Stands like a rock
Always impartial in judgement

Through thick and thin in every endeavour
Every generation living
Father's legacy

One who loves without expression
Personifies responsibilities
Has unmatched power in the world
A role model and a protector
A backbone of every family

Finally, God added all the qualities
A wisdom, strength, calmness, kindness, courage
Generosity, patience, faith, joy, love
Warmth, power and made a mould
To create a masterpiece
None other than a father.

Parvinder Nagi

THE IRONY OF LIFE

Are we really going through the irony of this life?

Yes, life is full of
Unexpected twists and turns
Leading to ironic situations
Ever striking fear for a fatherly figure

Understanding the values
And priorities of his family
Being open to the evolving
Nature of desires
And needs of his children

Father stepping forward
Towards dangling possibilities
To feed his children fishing in the deep seas
Life is not a game of arrows
Hitting the right point and
You easily win

Unveiling the obstacles
Yet the treat we are looking forward to
Our scrumptious fish meal
Whilst a fish is also having
A lust of feeding her own family

We are all so depending
Upon each other that keeps
Thrusting us into the depths of uncertainty
And challenging

The very essence of our being
In the interplay of dreams and fears
In the unceasing pursuit of purpose
To navigate the labyrinthine path

To unravel the mystery of ironic life

It is always the father
May be a human being or an Aquarius
Taking every lead and struggling
To suffice the hunger of his children

Life is mysterious force
Both tender and cruel
I would say it is
A master of irony of life.

Parvinder Nagi

TORMENTED DILEMMA

Have we ever realised
Embedded in our own
Evil thoughts
Lives our enemy

Building facades through our journey
Raging within our own self
Are the grudges and strifes
Sometimes our own weaknesses
Become our biggest enemies

Our own demons live
In the abyss of our hearts
Blowing away the winds of dust
From the mirror of reflections
Breaking the shards
Of our dreams

Tormented dilemma tears apart
Pondering over this predicament
Foreseeing the hidden truth
Where you stand
Your own enemy.

HEALING WOUNDS

Brimming with grief is my heart
For the wounds are sensitive
Scars not healed and
Aching is every breath

Tread softly across my soul
I fret not the realms of life
Living in the world of thoughts
So pure and true with profound start
Enhancing peace to the mind

When everything is lost
Inspiring spirit regenerating anew
Through the lilting winds
Fragrances brushing the cheeks
Bringing comfort to senses

It is now that matters
Healing wounds magnetically
Awakening the inner light
Embracing your soul forever.

TATTERED STRINGS

Dancing with orchestrated steps
Moving with the whims of spirit

Slowly manipulated with the magical strings
Perplexed by the shadows dark

Crafted exceptionally for toying back and forth
In the quiet realm of emotions

Through the cords they eternally play
On the diary's empty pages

The evil fate laughs endlessly
Tattered strings keep tuned

Pleasing the puppeteer
Abandoning the wooden limbs

In misfortune heartlessly
My everlasting fate lays

Hollow and wavering
With shadows grey.

SAILING THROUGH THE ROUGHEST STORMS

Life's roughest storms prove

The strength of your anchors

Diving in the deepest oceans

Sailing through the roughest weathers

Sometimes walking on the lonely shores

Wading through the waters calm and quiet

Sometimes moving through

The unreasonable expectations

With a sigh of tears

Wetting the pillow

Sobbing through the dark nights

Surfing over the crest of each wave

Transfixed in million thoughts

Crystallized in embraced moments

Losing and finding oneself

Through the scars

And scratches of life

Parvinder Nagi

Letting goes off the things

That cannot be changed

Let your path lead you

To the place

Where you belong.

FAREWELL TO WAR

Let there be peace
Why all the battles and wars?

Let the world symbolize peace
Where love and joy never cease
The world is torn apart
Needs eradication of sores and conflicts

It's heartening when the child asks, "Where's my school and
Where are my books?"

The timid girl asks, "Where's my food and where's the peace?"

Futures are lost and the dreams scattered
No answers are found to the unlimited queries of innocent faces
For tyrants have no mercy bringing the war with destruction
Ending the hopes for tomorrow

Killing thousands of innocent people rendered homeless
Victims of devastation for boundless greeds
There's erosion and explosion with agony of cries and screams
Roars of guns and bombs unleashing the blood so red
Leaving piles of lifeless bodies

Let solutions be found
Without delays or access of impediments
Let's bid farewell to war and glorify the earth
Let there be no More blood shed

Let the childhood, laughter and peace be back!

Parvinder Nagi

THE WHEEL OF LIFE

Holding secrets of the world
Rocking in the cradle galore
Life starts with silent giggles
Unfolding the life's stories

Embracing the childhood
Wrapping in the youth so subtle
Taking the flights of time
On the wings of dreams

Moving along the subtle life
With ups and downs like a merry-go-round
Sustaining every moment
Weaving the fabric of memories

Cherishing every bond
From childhood to getting old
Life is full of joys and sorrows
Sometimes be holding the soothing fragrances

And at times the fury storms
Sometimes tears and fears
At times sharing and caring
Dwelling through all the phases

Completing the cycle
With a sigh of last breath
Unto the bed
Of death.

THE SECRET LANGUAGE

A beautiful symphony across the miles
Listening to the rhythms of heart
We meet under the same clouds
Cascading emotions sublime and pure

Unspoken silence conveying the messages so divine
Entwining the souls in the world of dreams
Embracing each other
Through the bonding so strong

Mystical thoughts woven
In the tapestry of love notes
Whispering so gently
The secrets untold

Crossing the boundaries
Through the bridges of realm
The silent quill conveying
The messages so deep

Sailing through the seas
Floating on the waves
Connecting the souls
Kissing the dreams so wild

Where words silently connect
The secret language of mind
Listening to each other's heartbeat
Connecting heart to heart.

LIFE'S TAPESTRY

How do we weave
Life's silken tapestry
With satin linens
And lacy bounties
Embedding our thoughts
Into words of love

Shades of moods
Woven into memories
Emotions embroidered into
Gestures of speech
Decorated with sequins of smiles

Every stitch completing
A web of relations
Binding us together
Through the threads of trust
Making the bonds even stronger
Amongst the beautiful souls

Unfolding the knots of forgiveness
Discovering the patterns
Of kindness
The strands of fabric
Shaping life into
The golden fortune
Weaving life's silken tapestry.

TRANSCEND TIME

It's the time to talk to yourself
Immersed in your own thoughts
Feeling the breeze so cool
Sitting under the studded stars
Listening to your inner voice
Pure and serene
You are being you

Unedited is every thought
Serenity of quietness
Connected to yourself
Fear not the darkest night
For even the shadows tend to vanish
Succumbing to your own
Battles of mind

The measure of strength
Protecting you from the evil
Defeating the night gaze
Visualising the canvas
Painting your own escapades
For it's time to talk to yourself.

MADDENING POETRY

Here's the madness of poetry
Tangled in burgundy fringes
Dazzling in the romance of breeze
Lulled in the scintillating
Fragrance of locks
Imbibing the ambiguous
Magical mysteries
Unfolding the mystical strands
With flare and style
Drifting the rhythm of music
Unto the depths of horizon
Caressing strands of my hair
Enamoured with its fragrance
Plunged with intoxication
Glorious cascades soft and silky
Pleasingly tumbles down the neck
Twisting and turning curls
Enlightening my mood
Expression of woman's beauty
Strength to confidence
Be – holding the traces of love
Erranding the fingers
Through the enticing strands
Kissing the cheeks
Enhancing the scents
Whispering through the tresses
Full of enchantments
O' what an aromatic ecstasy
Is a maddening poetry.

A POET NEVER DIES

Breaking the shackles of time
Are the poets

Like the hero of fables
Expressing his thoughts
So confidently
Focusing his mind
Through the lens of words
Keeping you alive through
Every page pigmented with
Squiggles of his ink

He loves creating stories
Chasing silver moonbeams
Painting canvases so bright
Drenching you in
Fragrances so intoxicating
Taking you to the vistas unknown
For he is a logophile
Deep within his soul
You will find your place

Intricately weaving tapestry of life
Through his quill so fine
Connecting souls from
Every diversity
Enriching every imagination
Uniting the world
With manifestations divine

Magically weaving
A series of fictions and poetry
Within his embrace you will dwell
Swimming in the ocean
Of words

Parvinder Nagi

Finding the pearls so real
Fetching rewards
To his writings

An image of great authors
Writers and poets
Never fades
Projecting you through his quill
Keeping you in the bliss
Of his pages

A poet never dies
In his writings shall EVER live
Breathing through his ink
Living in his verses forever.

FRAGRANCE OF POETRY

Poetry is like the first love

Kissing all the alphabets

Here and there

Lingering with the essence

Of its perfume

Touched with the fragrance

Of emotions

Obsessed with metaphors

Rhymes and rhythms

Infatuating are the dreams

Floating on the clouds of fantasies

Revealing secrets of

The hidden desires

Balancing the beauty of

The naked verses.

Parvinder Nagi

A POEM IN A POEM

Deep inside a poem
Is a beautiful universe
Some secrets and some
Coded messages
Worth a Pearl in the ocean

A collection of 26 alphabets
Putting together into
Thoughts and verses
Interpretation of words
Strung together
Adding music to
A beautiful rendition

Most esoteric and treasured
Little collections of valued gems
Solacing your skin and soul
Each time you read
It speaks of different weathers
Drenching you in the aroma
Of pines in the woods

Drifting you to beliefs
Merging you into imaginations
Existing in the poem
Is the poet itself
Writing his conscious
And subconscious visions
Creating his poem in a poem.

MAGIC OF VERSES

Let us celebrate the magic of verses so beautiful!

Resonating like entwined strings
Weaving the stories so nostalgic
Spreading the beauty of its treasures
Through the bridges across the seas
Binding the nations with unity and peace

Whilst rearranging the sentences
Touching your senses with endless emotions
The quill of every poet
Weaving the dreams of his thoughts
Giving the literary meaning

Let the readers receive the seeds of knowledge
The exuberance of poetry
Leading to the new stories
Leading the literature
To the soaring skies so beautiful

The blossoms of quill
Revealing the mysteries of time
Intoxicating poetry
An ode to the loving hearts
Enriching the literature.

COVERS OF BOOKS

Between the covers of books
Are the mysterious stories hidden
In millions of bits of words
Discovering the strange world
From far lands and deep seas
Taking on ride to the galaxies vast
Are the magical chapters

Casting a magical spell
Where ghosts dwell
And witches troll
Where carpets fly
And Mermaids sing
In the fairylands
Dance the Fairy dust fairies

Through the pages
Travelling the oceans
Crossing the mountains
The brooks and the nooks
Rhymes and rhythms
The treasures are found
Through the library shelves
Between the covers of the books.

WORDS SO DEEP

Creeping candidly deep down
Words touch the core of your heart
Sometimes compelling you
To walk on the path of thorns
Hurting more than a wound
For words are powerful
Than the sword

In the fit of anger
It knows, how to bite and fight
Easily turns a friend into foe
Maliciously, leaving you
Rumbled and tumbled
Irreparable are the words once spilled

How do we reconcile time
When the words go silent
Transforming the emotions
Playing around with words
Like the lyrics of song
Stuck on a Gramophone record
Playing repeatedly

Words jolted and molted
Gushing through the mind
Haunting through the ages
Bringing your stories at halt
Leaving the pages blank
Over casting with vacuum
Magical, is the power of words

Sometimes, an enthralling bliss
For words are soothing balm
To the naked scars
Comforting your slayed brain

Parvinder Nagi

Apologies done and trusts built
Keeping promises at bay
Mending the broken hearts
And connecting the souls divine

Words can wring the tears
From the strongest hearts
Shattering your dreams
Ambiguous are the words
Only to be forgiven
And never to be forgotten

Therefore, be aware of the words
You choose.

INTEGRITY

A lifelong certification
A priceless reward valid until death
A rarest wealth
Giving purpose and yielding to the
Finesse results

Integrity leads to the paths
Shone with success
Choosing the light of truth
Where the world rife in darkness
We need a home to be known as paradise

Can we not have a planet
Safe with ecosystems?
Our motherland be safe
For sustenance
Our children would feel free
Where we all can breathe fearlessly

A power of tranquility
Preaching Gods high values
Searing the thrust of truth
Let the world be blessed
With the integrity that never
Goes unnoticed.

HARMONISING SUCCESS OVER THE FAILURE

Lurking in the shadows
Are the fears of past
A light of hope glimmering
Amid failure
Dreams unfulfilled
Struggles unsuccessful
Living in disappointment
And bizarre

Walking hand in hand
Success and failure
Learning from mistakes
Of each other
Saying goodbyes
To the bends of life
Adding joy to the
Paths anew

Mending the pieces
Through the gentle thoughts
Never to give up
The melancholy of success
Touching some ephemeral endings
Harmonizing success
Over the failure.

MY EMPTY CHAIR

Scuffling the heat, the earth bears
Toiling the fields with scars of tan

Here comes the drizzling
Of pouring rain
Gazing upon the glory
Of beauty unfold
Singing thunder songs
Creating the
Havoc of wonders

The calmness of ocean, drowning
My sorrows deep.
Each wave giving a message
Nothing is forever
Everything that comes
Must vanish away

The bed of stars beautifully sewn
In the Sky, the myriads of splendours
Loved so fondly
Little reminders of Forget - me- nots
In the dark blanket of night
Witnessing your majesty

The queen of night shines
On the harbour quays
Blooming with her silver crown
Assuring us as it glows
Nudging us to the next sunrise
For every end
Has a beautiful beginning

One fine day all will be gone
That message in an empty bottle

Dry flowers in the page of my book
The withered bluebells
Down the windowsill
The dreams unfulfilled

Beckoning my days past
My stories untold
My songs unsung
Birds will sing my blues away
And the winds will caress
My empty chair

Would life not love me again?

THE LAST STAMP

A unique pain of grief
Is taking place
Nothing is same as ever before

The bereaved emotions are bottled deep down
Counting on to vent out
Any day, any hour, any minute, any second
The shadows dark is casting over
Bothering me why only you were chosen
To go through this suffering so scary

Together we grew up
Challenging the tough times of life
Listening to our favorite gems
From the golden era
Sleepovers and late-night chats
Making precious memories
From India to overseas

Enjoyed lavish treats you took us for
Loved travelling in your company
Through underground tubes
Escorting to the finest shopping centres
And London tourisms

Untiringly walking across the bridges
Over the river Thames
Oxford Street, Regent Street
Perfume shops and Souvenir
Having to hold my shoes in hands
Hurting my feet
Yet not giving up walking

How strong you had been then
Now suffering through the deep pain

Without a moan to the almighty
Fighting your wounds
All by yourself with all the aches
Were you really supposed to go
Through the unbearable agony beyond words?

My heart is sinking
My eyes are moistened
Holding this beautiful RAKHI
Meant to be ornamented on your weak wrist
Letting you know that I miss you loads
Living miles away across the seas

Hope I am not writing your ADDRESS
For the LAST TIME!

May this not be the "LAST STAMP"

On this precious envelope
Carrying your sister's love!

YOU LOSE NOT JUST ONCE

This poem is a tribute to my brother
Who fought cancer till his last breath
And now he is no more

When you lose someone
You lose not just once!

You lose them every moment
You lose in the silence
When no one is around
When your mind is wandering
Waking up in the morning
Finding them nowhere

An empty chair not pulled
A cup of tea not filled
A toast not buttered
And so you lose them
On the breakfast table too

You lose them in the studded sky
When the day settles in the dusk
And dawn awakens

You lose them on every celebration
Birthdays, weddings and holidays too
And for all the special dates
You celebrated with them

You lose them for they are no more with you
...In frames
...In albums
...In notes
...In diaries

You lose them not once
But you lose them everyday
For the pair of shoes
Not picked
Spectacles not used
A wallet not opened

You lose them when you listen
To their favourite songs
Fragrances of perfumes
Reminding of their absence

You lose them in the places
You visited along
In the conversations you did
And the decisions you made

You lose them everyday
On the calls no more done
Routines no more shared
For the gifts no more sent
For the address no more prevails

You lose them when the seasons change
The snow falls
The flowers bloom
The rain comes
The leaves fall
The wind blows

You lose them when you realise the reality of life

You lose them picking up the broken pieces of your relationship

You lose them no matter how much
You miss them
And need them

Pray for them
But they will never come back

You lose them repeatedly
For days to go
Months to come
Year after year
For all the memories unfading

You lose them until you age yourself
With blurry memories
Gracious greys proving
Your age
Walking with support

The face watching you out
From a faded old photo
Once you knew
Once you loved

You lose not someone just once

You lose them over repeatedly

Memories haunting
Through the rest of your life.

FINAL DESTINATION

(A tribute to my elder brother)

For dust you are
And to dust you shall return!

Now that you are gone
Limousine carrying
Your cadaver has arrived
Family and friends
Gathered from far and near
Consoling each other
Accepting the final truth
No longer the bond
That we shared
You were incredibly SPECIAL
Now laid to rest
In this coffin
On the weak wrist
My Rakhi tied
My letter read to you
By my younger sister
And placed
Into your pocket
To be carried with you
How emotional is that
The funeral flowers offered
The final prayers said
The final rituals done
The tributes given
The messages read
The last procession
The last journey
On this earth

The FINAL DESTINATION

Has arrived
The undefeated truth
Leaving a message
Nothing is forever
Everything that comes
Must vanish away
Here I bow my head
To mark a respect
The tears I cannot hide
And the pain
Within my heart
You did not go alone
For part of us
Went with you.

Parvinder Nagi

THE LAST FULFILMENT

Ah! here's death
The last fulfilment of life

Death be a beautiful sadness
A deep sleep-in disguise

As we believe it is something
mighty and dreadful

Death is a pathway
To eternal life's journey

Life and death are inseparable
Yet loved and lost

Life is full of curdled manifestation
Of dreams and hopeful delusions

Where death brings in panicking confusions
Ending up the jolting hopes

Deciphering the old chapters
Sprouting life anew.

COLORS OF HUES

Morning comes with beautiful compassion
Adorned by waves of summer breeze
Where intoxicated perfume of flowers stays
Adorning the beauty of everyday life

Sun rays fill the souls serene
Nature's mysteries prevail on canvas so beautiful
Gently caressing the trances magical
Lovers stand amidst placidity

Surrounded by nature's love
The beautiful morning adorns
Painted with colours of hues
Glowing with richness of heavenly rays

The sun kisses every petal so delicate
Dancing in Gods glory
Singing to the natures choir
My heart loves the wonders of hues.

PRISTINE MOMENTS

Living my life in the moment
Which never comes back
As every new dawn
Brings me a blank canvas
To sprinkle the essence
Of my desires
Where I sing evermore
With no apologies

Every note depicting my
Gracious mood
Soothing sensations
And urge aligned
In the moment of momentum
Unaltered sequence of thoughts
Bringing tranquility and empathy

Weaving harmony and melody
Countering my blank gaze
Not knowing the dynamics of annui
Amid the bits of world

The musical strings dancing
To and fro like the pendulum of a clock
Pure are the concoctions of mind
Twisting and twirling on the rhythm of life
I dance tapping on my own beat
Through the pristine moments
Of the divine journey of my life.

HEAVENLY GLORIES

Miraculous night celebrating
Heavenly glories
With intoxicating adorations
Embracing heavens
Decorating the skies with
Galaxies of diamonds

Wrapped into one
And the moonlit night looks
Like a bride in the linen veil
The misty air so intoxicating
Clouds wandering in them
Playing peekaboo
With the mystic moonbeams
Dancing in pride

Are we too going to be the part
Of these Illuminated celebrations one fine day?

Oh, are we
Waiting for the heavens
Fascinating invites?

For no one is having an escape
From the destined moments
No illusions no myths
Leaving behind
The pandemonium
Just admire the heavenly abode
Mesmerising in the royal gaze
With finest celestial decorum
Almighty's enthralling beauty

With incandescent lamps
Dispelling all the

Darkness of your life
Once for ever
Unlocking the secrets

Here we rest our minds
Hearts and souls
Saying one final goodbye
To the earth
Always gazing and jealous
With its bewitching charms
Admiring silently
The glorious celebrations
And heavenly decors of
The glistening night.

GLISTENING MOONBEAMS

Weaving the tapestry of dreams
Under the gleaming moon
Crafting the realms unknown
She wanders in her reflections blue

Beneath the silvery embrace of moon
Bonding in the crystals blue
Sailing across the ambles of shore
Lying under the silver gleams

Singing her tales of ecstasy
In mystical ways through the breeze so gentle
Dreaming her fancies
She dances under the moonlit sky

Bathed in the glistening moonbeams
Weaving the tapestry of love beneath the horizons vast
Kissing the gentle breeze so cool
Silently embracing the threads of love

Rumbling and tumbling she goes
Whirling in her blue fabric
Cascading through the sparkling night
Wrapped in enchanting secrets holding
A silver trance through the stillness of night.

FASCINATING NATURE

Away from the clamour of hustles

The tranquility of countryside
The lilies dancing in the
Coherent rhythms
The enhancing beauty of nature
Moonbeams kissing
Every object of nature
Night is reigned with the
Calmness, relieving stress
Enlivens your senses
Comforting your souls
Clothed in the dazzling silver robes
Bathed in the moonlight rays
The flowers swaying
In the cool breeze
Emitting sweet fragrances
The petals dancing to the
Tune of whispering willows
Moon the night queen
A splendour among the
Fascinating landscapes
Every object cheerful
Rendering to the mirthful
Fascinating spectacle
A feast to the eyes.

FRAGMENTS OF SUMMER NIGHT

In the fragments of night
Through the willows so bright
Comes the dark night of June
Liberating the fragrances of new season afresh

Through the capturing blue azures
Whispering secrets of new stories
Lilting the midnight ecstasies
Diffusing aromas of summer air

Whistling through the leaves so green
Are the breezes so gusty and warm
Here comes the downpour of rain
Awaited by everyone
Bringing relief to the thirsty souls

The mystical jaded moon playing hide and seek
Through the clouds so grey and meek
Missing you between the silver moonbeams
I wish to cuddle you under the summer sky so beautiful

Inhibitions gone in a blink
Pondering through the horizon of thoughts
Synchronizing the unknown heartbeats
Playing with the rhythms of symphony

Chasing the summer night dreams
The frail dazzling stars across the sky like a flowing river
Resonating the bed linens with scents of your body
I stay intoxicated lying under the celestial carpet of summer night.

THE ENCHANTING MOON

In the soft stillness of night
Waiting to look upon
Your dazzling beauty
Beyond the expressions of words

You are the celestial beauty
A magnificent power
The intense creation
Surrounded by innumerable stars

Spreading magical rays
Symbolizing love in many forms
Inspiring the lovers
Ruling over their emotions

A mystery full of aspirations
Eroding the darkness
Across the skies
Elevating the night zone

Enlightening the universe
A compassionate wooer
Enchanting companion
Loyal forever

Painting the world silver
Ruling over the night
Weak and wan sometimes
You tickle millions of hearts

A lover's paradise
Radiance so divine
A fantasy in the galaxy
Drifting beyond the skies
Harmonizing the desires

A celestial symphony
Walking down the aisle of moonbeams
With hundreds of secrets

Inconvincible mystery
Yet bonding together
Unknown relationships
Forever and ever.

RHYTHMS OF HEART

Binding the strings of heart
In mellifluous notes
Singing your name
Embedded in every verse of my poetry
Captivating your emotions
With grace and love
I hear the rhythms
Of your heart so warm

You will be hummed in every lyric
Of my verse so fine
Painting your world anew
Never letting you fall apart
I assure you for the lifetime
Keeping forever entwined
Your heart with mine

Upholding the emotions thine
Blending the moments sublime
Twinning the hearts
I will make you live in the
Stories divine

Submerging in the
Mystic spirit of my soul
You are the threshold
In the path of my life
My world gets transferred
Into the beautiful realms
As I conquer the treasures
Of your love.

PAINT YOUR DREAMS

Love your life
To enhance its beauty
For one day when you will get up
There will not be enough time
To do the things you always
Wished to

You are an artist
Who can evade the verbose
Femininity is the love
Of your radiance
Dignity and strength

It's not the hairdos
And trendy clothes but
An adornment of your
Behaviour and qualities

It is the creativity
And an expression of your actions
Accept the challenges
Doing trivial things
In a profound way
And paint your dreams
With graciousness.

Parvinder Nagi

UNTO THE DEPTHS OF DARKNESS

Each day nearing to the
Ripped pages of a book
Drowning down
The depths of gloom
One day forever
To be lost and forgotten

Flying on the
Broken wings of time
Mending the wounds
Of the past
Searching for contentment
In discontent decisions made

Living in flashbacks
Collecting the broken pieces
With grief of haunting memories
Through the stings of pain
Unto the depths
Of darkness.

SHADOWS OF REALMS

In the life's tapestry are the shadows of realms
Celestial path guiding with a positive aspect

When mysteries dwell in the darkness of clouds
No wonder the lights of galaxies illuminates

The world so beautiful
Embracing the dusk of night

Greys are the blessings in disguise
Brightening the path with stars

Reminding of the resilience and vulnerability
Greeting each morning

With sunshine so bright
Weaving the fabric of hopes

Bringing melodies so sweet
Cherishing all the moments

Through the positive aspect
Every cloud that brings.

Parvinder Nagi

MELANCHOLIC BEAUTY

Here's the melancholic beauty of night
Where the shimmering stars
Spread the blanket of their shadows

Moon the mistress of night
Whispering sweet symphonies
Mysterious body shrouded in dark mysteries

Untold Secrets and hidden stories
Painful yet unseen woes
Through the undefined paths so dark

Unable to embrace the shadows grey
Yet a beacon of hope
Guiding the travellers with light so bright

Struggling the battle playing hide and seek
Behind the clouds so grey
Like joys and sorrows in the realm of life.

GRATITUDE TO THE GLORIES OF GOD

Let's be thankful for the paths
We have walked in harmony
For the trees comforting
In the scorching heat
And the birds chirping making
Our world so beautiful

Let's be thankful for the
Glorious hues of sky above
And the refreshing grass
Beneath our feet
The amazing joys of universe
Leaving us amazed

Let's be thankful for our life
Full of splendour and
Filled with joys tender
Subtle breeze touching the skin
Gladdening the sublime hearts

Let's be thankful and raise the
Notes of almighty's praise
The supreme power's
Fulfilment and rich opportunities
Rare are who cherish gathering
The rosebuds with gratitude.

AN ELOQUENT WOMAN WITH MAJESTIC AURA

Yes, I deserve to be celebrated
For who I am today

I have woven the fabric of my life
Through the colourful patchwork
Adorning my journey
Through paths so rough
Paving through
The rusty weather so tough

Sewing every little patch of my life
I have crossed the milestones
Accomplishing my dreams

Unveiling into every charm
Celebrating my femininity
I walk under the celestials
Carrying my enchanting aura

Binding the verses of poetry
Woven with the threads
Of golden tapestry
I live in glamour
Shining across
The paths so beautiful

Unfolding the stories
In myriads of ways
I am the finesse fragrance
Of God's glory
Unwrapped mystery
With majestic aura
An embodiment

Of love and light

They say I am a magical wonder

Yes! there's definitely more to me

In the stillness
Of my soothing mind
In the awakening presence
Of my own kind
Fulfilling my ethereal
Dreams so precious

I am an eloquent woman
With majestic aura.

Parvinder Nagi

ABOUT THE AUTHOR

"Weaving my memories
Into a secret story
Finding few lines of poetry
Through the ink of my quill."

— Parvinder Nagi

Parvinder Nagi was born and raised in the vibrant coastal city of Mombasa, Kenya, East Africa, where her early connection with the natural world and the rhythmic tides of the ocean nurtured her creative spirit. After migrating to India, Parvinder pursued a distinguished career in education, serving as the principal of prestigious senior secondary schools. Her leadership and innovative pedagogical approaches left a lasting impact on both her students and colleagues.

Parvinder's deep love for art and creativity has always been at the core of her multifaceted personality. From winning accolades in portrait making to her contributions in the field of education, she has continuously pushed the boundaries of her talents. It is this same creative energy that flows into her poetry, where she explores universal themes of life, love, and the human experience.

Her journey into the world of poetry took a profound turn during a visit to Dove Cottage, the home of William Wordsworth in Grasmere, UK. Immersed in the rich literary history, Parvinder found herself inspired by the legacy of one of the great romantic poets, a moment that became the catalyst for her own poetic endeavors.

Parvinder's poetry has been recognized and celebrated internationally, with her works translated into various languages and featured in global anthologies. Her ability to capture life's emotions—from joy to sorrow—through evocative imagery and lyrical expression has resonated with readers across the world.

A poet, educator, and lifelong learner, Parvinder continues to weave her love for the arts into everything she does. Whether through her writing, travels, or other creative pursuits, she stays dedicated to exploring the beauty of life and sharing it through the art of poetry.

Parvinder Nagi
(Principal)

ACKNOWLEDGMENT

As I reflect on the journey that has brought me to this moment, I am reminded of the sensitive and passionate child I once was— always in tune with the rhythms of the universe. I have always believed that humanity is deeply interconnected, each of us meeting one another in some way, spreading energy and positive vibrations.

Life is a tapestry of experiences, some filled with joy and others marked by disagreements, disappointments, and heartache. Each soul carries its own story. We must navigate these varied emotions, learning to forgive without necessarily forgetting, moving forward into new beginnings with the wisdom of the past still with us.

For me, poetry has always been a means of capturing life's ebb and flow—painting the horizon of existence with carefully chosen words, pouring meaning into every emotion and syllable. Since my college days, I have found solace in writing small verses that reflect the many colors of nature. These pearls of wisdom, adorned with the visions of my heart, have shaped my journey.

The poems in this collection are entirely my own creations, born from the sea of my thoughts, flowing in harmony with the supreme forces of nature—the countryside, the brooks, the meadows, and the memories. These emotions find their way into verses, capturing both the traumas and joys of daily life, and serving as a reminder of the natural gifts bestowed upon us. I am forever thankful to the Almighty for His pure light that illuminates even the shadows of our "empty chair."

I am eternally grateful to my family and my twin daughters Ketty and Betty, who have been my pillars of strength. Their unwavering support and belief in me have been the driving force behind this work. I could not have completed this journey without their endless encouragement and love.

I am forever indebted to my brilliant, loving, and caring son Manpinder Singh Nagi for his unwavering support, who stood by me as a rock, with boost of confidence and like a Euneirophrenia who made a real difference in fulfilling my dreams, making this book 'UNFATHOMED SECRETS' a reality.

Deepest gratitude to my loving and wonderful daughter-in-law Mansi Nagi for love and kind support in every aspect making my poetic journey carry out magnanimously.

To my dear husband, Mr. Gurbachan Singh Nagi, my deepest gratitude for his patience, time, and his constant support, which allowed me the freedom to complete this book.

A special and heartfelt thanks to the world-renowned author, professor, and noble poetess, **Gordana Saric**—the Queen of Poetry—whose unwavering guidance and inspiration has touched me deeply. Without her support, this book would have still been incomplete.

Lastly, I am deeply grateful to all those who have crossed my path and shared their pearls of wisdom along the way. Your influence has been invaluable to me.